POPULAR HOME REMEDIES AND SUPERSTITIONS

OF THE PENNSYLVANIA GERMANS

First Edition 1941
A. Monroe Aurand Jr.

Original foreword by
Logan Clendening M.D.

New Edition 2020
Edited by Tarl Warwick

COPYRIGHT AND DISCLAIMER

FOREWORD

This little booklet is a very good compilation of folklore related to the Pennsylvania German community. The end of the book contains a valuable bibliography which actually lists two different occult works I myself have edited; "Pow Wows" by Hohman and Magnus' "Egyptian Secrets." As expected, both of these technical Petit-Albert style bric-a-brac quasi-grimoires were semi-secretly kept by many of the same folks in that region.

The folklore is very interesting; much as with any other culture there are three main concerns with regards to it- human mortality, romance, and general luck. Some of the entries here are provided a quick aside by the author, who clearly does not believe literally in the folklore itself, as many of the folk living in the area did (and sometimes, still do.) It is an interesting facet of such localized folklore that it persists even now nearly a century later- some of it is not strictly and solely from the Pennsylvania Dutch (the idea of a married couple "jumping the broom" or the belief in black cats being unlucky are common in many areas and among many people) and all of it is fascinating.

It should be noted that such folkloric compilations were extremely popular in that era and that part of that was due to a strong longing towards civic identity.

This edition of "Popular Home Remedies and Superstitions of the Pennsylvania Germans" has been carefully edited for format and content. Care has been taken to retain all original intent and meaning.

POPULAR HOME REMEDIES AND SUPERSTITIONS OF THE PENNSYLVANIA GERMANS

PERTINENT!

The men in the shops, in the fields, in the offices; the professional men and the tots in school, ought to, and must be made more fully acquainted with their coming into the community through a generous and right-thinking ancestry; and there is no more profitable, agreeable and consistent way in which this education of the people can be accomplished, than through an applied study and. reading of such books as local history, in all the schools and homes of the country. If the achievements of those of the pioneer days are not worthy of mention and study at this day and age, of how much less value and appreciation will our' labors appear to those of a not-far-off-tomorrow?

FOREWORD TO THE 1941 EDITION

My friend. Mr. Aurand. has been interested in superstitions for a long time, and apparently because he lives in a hot-bed of them, he has been able to collect a great many curious examples of them.

This has always appealed to me because 1 am interested in superstitions also, but I think I have a somewhat different view towards them than Mr. Aurands. Our differences are not very easy to express. Mr. Aurand obviously believes that all superstitions are without foundation and very funny examples of the deviations of the human intellect. It must be admitted that most of the examples he has collected support this view.

But somewhere in the back of my mind, or perhaps we had better say somewhere in the back of my emotions, I have a feeling that superstition is the mother of science. I am not at all dogmatic about this and am willing to modify it to say "some superstitions" are the mother of science.

Of course, a very definite example is that of the milk-maids of Gloucestershire, who believed that if they rinsed their milk pails with scalding water before milking, it would prevent the milk from souring. This idea was an object of scorn by all the scientists who ever heard of it, including John Hunter. Unquestionably, the idea that walking under a ladder is bad luck could be proved statistically. I don't suppose there is any really good support for the ingrained opinion that the possession of a two dollar bill is bound to be worked out in sweat and blood, but I notice that the Treasury Department has quit printing them. What interests me is not so much why other people believe their own superstitions, but why I believe mine. It just so happens that I fall for the two dollar bill credence and upon the occasion of a series of dire misfortunes that befell me in the Upper part of Wisconsin about 1915. I went out into the night and placed a two dollar bill under a rock near a pine tree on the shores of Plum Lake. It is probably there yet. But I do know that the next day the clouds lifted and the troubles vanished and when recently in Santiago de Chile an expatriate American tried to give me a two dollar bill in exchange for Argentine money, I refused even to touch the hem of the bill.

I retain a few other superstitions. Enough to be quite sympathetic toward those who cherish the ones that I do not happen to subscribe to. As I examine the matter as a problem in psychology, I conclude that the superstitions that were held in your own household were so drummed into you in childhood, that you never were able to get over them. All the more credit then, to the conquests you have made of a few superstitions. I take almost as much pride in the fact that I no longer consider Friday or thirteen as unlucky, as I do in my Sigma Psi key. Mr. Aurand's collection is amusing and unique. The mere reading of it makes for liberty of the intellect. But don't forget that some of them may be the real McCoy.

LOGAN CLENDENING, M. D.
Kansas City, Mo.

"HOME REMEDIES" AND "SUPERSTITIONS"

For a long time we have been an interested observer of the behavior of man as a member of society. We have noticed him in his every day walks of life; in his home and office; on his farm and in his church. One man will do one thing one way, while some other man will do it another way- we know these things, but the odd part of it is that if these other fellows have the right way- (which is right)- why don't we follow suit? No, we are afraid that there isn't any "right" way- other than the way they can best perform and best agree.

The facts presented in this account cannot be accepted point blank as a panacea for any individual or public ills. When you look upon a mirror squarely you see what you see, and herein we likewise reflect and present those things as they have come to us out of the past.

It is hardly fair to assume that because we have listed a number of oddities that we favor them, or object to them. In the experience of life one learns to respect the opinions and likes of others, in public utterances- quite often to rail about them in private! Our collection seems to border largely on "home remedies," developed before the days of physicians, and certainly long before science was a recognized force or philosophy. The condition of one who is ill always preys on the minds of loved ones, as to whether recovery may be counted on; hence no limits to reason may be expected. Religions are like that, and prayers short and long, silent and wordy, are constantly used throughout the world for recovery from illness, and for other "wants."

Thus the weight of religious "responsibilities" and "home economy" are so interwoven in the lives of men that one cannot determine what it is that brings about recovery- prayer, or right nourishment. Of one thing we are sure- "sympathy" is one thing in life, which, if supplied and conveyed at the right time and place, will do as much or more good than prayers and the "medicine" together. "Where there is any religion, the devil will plant superstition," says Burton, in "The Anatomy of Melancholy"- and it must be assumed that there is great difficulty in determining where one stops and the other starts. Is it reasonable on the one hand to say we have "angels" but no "witches"?

Are we right in concluding that most human ills are caused, if not primarily by wrong eating, then by "superstition," which means "excessive fear of the gods; unreasonable religious belief"? "The Century Dictionary," which we quoted, also says that "superstition" is: An ignorant or irrational fear of that which is unknown or mysterious; especially, such fear of some invisible existence or existences; specifically, religious belief or practice, or both, founded on irrational fear or credulity; excessive or unreasonable religious scruples produced by credulous fears. We leave it to the reader to say whether or not he doesn't know of cases that have been made "well," and others "ill," through a psychosis which is religious- or, in other words, that which is founded on fear and superstition. Which is which, by the way? Study a comprehensive dictionary some time, and determine for yourself how much you are involved in this thing we call "superstition"- which leads to fear and sickness of all sorts defying any comprehensive and understandable description.

"A superstition, as it's name imports, is something that has been left to stand over, like unfinished business, from one session of the world's witenagemot to the next," says Lowell, in "Among My Books," first series, p. 92.

When will we reach a state of "finished business" so that man will know that he is doing the right thing, the right way? The "time" element then will be nil.

CHILDHOOD AND ITS DEMANDS ON MAN

The depth of the love of a mother primarily, and of a father, for their child- no matter what race, creed or color- is something ever so natural. Procreation and birth come at a great risk and sacrifice, braving an indeterminate myriad of dangers from the cradle to the grave. These create in the hearts and minds of mothers all the fears, emotions and expectancy in the catalog of life's experiences.

Whether children are reared with care, or indifferently, there are always some phases of "ritual" they must pass through before they can create their own kind- and in their turn assume these "worries." Mothers "worry" about their babies as long as either live. While children go through the certain changes from birth until they can shift for themselves many exigencies develop, and these are met with by many notions and requirements which may, or may not. have the desired effect in times of sickness, etc. Let us examine, then, some of the odd beliefs and sayings about Childhood, brought down to us from "long ages:"

Baptismal Water- When several teaspoonfuls of its own baptismal water are given to a child, it will tend to make it "bright," and perhaps a good singer.

Births- How many of us recall that a person born in January can see ghosts?

A man who had the "luck" to be born in Pisces is usually thirsty.

If a child is born during a thunderstorm it will be killed by lightning. (A child born during a snow-storm- does it freeze to death?)

POPULAR HOME REMEDIES AND SUPERSTITIONS

To Cry- Immediately after birth a child should cry, or be slapped until it does.

Diaper- Put an old diaper on a new-born child, or it might become a thief. Or, it cannot stool easily. (Wonder how many of us were dressed "properly" the first day?) Burn the first diaper for luck.

Dress- The doctor, or mid-wife, or whoever, should always use care to place the child's right arm in the sleeve first. (This custom is centuries old, probably being Jewish in origin, and has much to do with being right, or left-handed in after years, and likewise with witches or evil spirits.)

The first dress put on a child should be new; an old one will cause it to be a "slop." (This sort of thing finds a continuation in the adult practice of having new clothes at Easter, or, as in the case of the Jews, at their New Year.)

Freckles- Rain drops on a child under a year will cause freckles. To get rid of them in after years, requires rising early in the morning of a certain day, and washing the face with dew from the grass.

Garret- A child on its first day should be carried to the garret (attic) and allowed to look out a garret window if it is to become a respected citizen. There are many rules about the things one must do on the child's first day.

Growth- To step over a child lying on the ground, or on the floor; to permit a child to crawl, or walk between a man's legs, or crawl in or out of windows- is said to stunt, or retard its growth. (There is a rule that, having crawled out through the window, one must crawl back again to "break the spell".)

Payment of the doctor's fee in full will prevent a child from growing.

POPULAR HOME REMEDIES AND SUPERSTITIONS

Frequent stretching out on the bare floor will aid young folks to attain greater length.

Hair- Children born with long hair will die early unless it soon falls out.

Horseshoe- Place a horseshoe with nails in it in a child's cradle; it is conducive to good health. (Keep the nails away from the child.)

Kiss- Please don't kiss a baby on its mouth before it cuts its teeth- it will teethe hard. (If it is kissed too much by those who may be offensive to it, it is defenseless to protect itself, as when it once has teeth!) A child, if kissed too much in its younger days, may suffer through a lack of the same in its older days.

Livergrown- If a child was livergrown, or seemed to have a spell, it was put three times through a horse-collar, taken from a horse, still warm. Good also for wind colic, or gripes. Lay a livergrown child on a door sill and measure it. When the child has outgrown this measure the complaint will also be forgotten.

Nursing- To guard against a child being left-handed it must be nursed the first time at the right breast.

Rocking the Cradle- To rock the cradle while empty will cause a child to lose its sleep, or may cause colic; or perhaps it will be livergrown.

Sleeplessness- An open Holy Bible under the pillow of a sleepless child, the mother placed

> ..."and there is treasure kept,
> While one short, fervent, prayer she said,
> And lo! her darling sweetly slept I"

POPULAR HOME REMEDIES AND SUPERSTITIONS

Smile- A smile on the face of a sleeping child may be a sign of colic. It may also be a sign that angels may be playing with it. Also, it may wake up soon- quite fretful and crabbed.

Stammer- To tickle a child before it is a year old may cause it to stammer.

Takeoff; (Abnahme; Obnemma)- There is a record of a Scotch-Irishman who applied three live lice to his child afflicted with malnutrition. The child is said to have improved.

Talking- On the day a child is born, husband and wife should not say much to each other. (Is it to "save the child," give the mother rest, or prevent the husband from saying things which would prove him, for the time being, of being "irrational"?) (The story is told about the man who mistrusted his wife. On an occasion she gave birth to twins. His suspicions were not easily allayed, and he continued to rant about the twins, declaring he recognized one of them, but that the other was "a stranger.")

Teeth- A child born with teeth will not live long.

Umbilical Cord- A child will become great and popular if born with the umbilical cord around its neck. When the cord is handed to a girl or boy in their 'teens, should the former sew it up, she will become a seamstress; if a boy cuts it into bits in any way, he'll turn out to be a wood-chopper.

Cord lore goes back many centuries- "save the umbilical cord for luck." (This custom is well known among the Jews.)

Urine- Washing the face of a child with urine of its own manufacture is said to make it handsome. Adult women in central Pennsylvania have been known to use this liquid for the purpose of beautification. (Urine is used by certain people to wash their hair; by certain Spanish people to cleanse their teeth; by the Esquimaux to wash their hands, face and body; by the

POPULAR HOME REMEDIES AND SUPERSTITIONS

Holland Dutch to give a special tint to cheese; and by some in the southern part of America to give tobacco a "good" aroma.)

Freckles may be taken away with urine washings.

Visiting- A baby taken out of doors for its first visit to the home of a newly married couple may cause the newlyweds to soon have a child of their own.

To Wean- If a child is weaned during the summer, it will die young. If weaned when the trees are in blossom, its hair will turn gray early, should there be still some snow on the ground. If weaned when the leaves fall, it will become bald.

FOLK MEDICINE AND OLD SUPERSTITIONS

"One man's meat is another man's poison," goes an old saying. Perhaps none of the following recipes would do you any good; we don't know whether they have ever done anyone any good, but when they were more or less generally in use they were the "next best thing" in the absence of what we now know as "physicians."

What, with all the hundreds of thousands of complaints of man, actual and imagined, we do not hesitate to say that doubtless some of these "cures" were as beneficial as some of the sugar-coated bread pills we pay out good money for, when we get them from our doctor, or druggist. When man is sick, or complains enough, there are no end of cures awaiting him, whether he goes to the M. D., or whether he depends entirely on the home remedies.

Finally, in desperation, man does anything- verything, as we may read.

Ague- If you would get "shut" of the ague drink of your own urine.

POPULAR HOME REMEDIES AND SUPERSTITIONS

Bedsores- If you lay the ax under the bed it may prevent bedsores; if you have no ax, draw a picture of one!

Bedwetting- A child that is more or less an habitual bedwetter should "piddle" into a grave covered that day; time, after dusk.

Fried mouse, or mouse pie, cures bedwetting; also, if burned to ashes, and the ashes secretly put into coffee, tea, or other drink, will cure. (We know of an actual case of the latter.)

Catarrah- Catarrah, one thing that most of us have more or less, (like the "possibilities" of a cold), can be cured, (it is said), by snuffing one's own urine at night, being sure to spit it out.

Cold in Head- This is an old, old cure: Pass your finger over your "hind-end" and smell it. For cold in head and chest, we know of a case where fresh hog dung was steamed and the vapor inhaled by a very sick patient in the upper part of Dauphin county, who had been "given up" by the doctor; the patient recovered, much to the surprise of all, and later it appears in medical circles that there was more than a little bit of merit in the cure. (Is any extreme merited to save a life?)

Constipation- (We like this cure): Get a chicken, nice or otherwise, kill it without shedding blood; boil it, feathers and all- make soup out of it- this, when eaten, will cure constipation.

Corns- Rub a candle on a corpse, then on the corn.

Drunkenness- If you scrape the dirt collected under his fingernails and put same into whiskey, which the drunkard will gladly drink, it will cure him of his nasty habit.

Emetic- Take the leaves of boneset, stripped upwards, and made into tea if you need an emetic; if the leaves are stripped downward, you have a purgative.

Epilepsy- To cure, swallow the heart of a rattle-snake.

Erysipelas- Lately the doctors have found out what erysipelas really is, but they do little for it. "Pow wow" on the one hand, or a salve made of sheep tallow, scrapings from elder and goose dung, are said to cure.

Another cure: take the patient's urine to a witch doctor.

Eye- To remove a foreign substance from the eye, or ease itching or smarting, rub the other eye. (This never irritates the affected part, and gives it some sympathetic attention.) If water from the first snow of winter is used, it is good for sore eyes.

Felon- If you place your finger between the door and the jamb, and someone closes the door, it will cure the felon.

Freckles- Remove freckles by washing them with the water of baptism. Or, with water collected from tombstones. If it rains on you while there is a rainbow, you will get freckles. Wash freckles with dew on the first of May.

Goosegrease- This property is said to be good for almost any ailment.

If you step on a nail, rusty or not, put the nail into fat, and keep in a dry place. If you cut yourself with anything metallic, grease affected part, and the offending object, and lay latter carefully away.

For a sty, "pow-wow" with a greasy plate.

Headache- If you would prevent headache, or toothache, you must form the habit of putting on your right stocking, first;

your right shoe, etc.

During dog-days, if rain falls on your head, look out for baldness, or headache.

Hernia- To reduce it use a sadiron. Another cure: Get a forged nail, drive it in wood, and keep in a dry place.

Hiccoughs- For this uncomfortable and annoying disturbance, sit down, with a glass of water by your side; let some one put a little water in each ear with the little finger of each hand, keeping the fingers there until you have drunk all the water.

Another: Bend forward so that the hands touch the ground and say: "O hiccough, I wish that you were in my buttocks."

The author had hiccoughs for five days during the epidemic of the early 1920's. After doctors had given up, he, having then tried many home remedies, became quite tired and worn out, was about to go to a hospital to die, like many others. He then decided to try the good old remedy for many ills- castor oil. Presto; with the first action of this oil relief came for the first time in five days. It would be interesting to see a list of the cures sent to doctors and hospitals when publicity is given to hiccough patients who do not respond to ordinary treatment- What is "ordinary" treatment?

Hives- Rub yourself on the pigs' litter if you would stop hives.

Homesickness- If you have a garden, take a pinch of ground from the cross path and put into coffee for homesickness. Another cure: For women, sew salt and bread into petticoats; for men, sew salt in a seam of the clothing.

POPULAR HOME REMEDIES AND SUPERSTITIONS

Drain coffee through a dish-cloth.

To keep a servant from leaving: put some of the scrapings from the door-sill into his or her food.

Hysteria- This is old-fashioned, but good: Pass your finger between your toes and smell it. This remedy may also be used for colds. (Do not run your fingers between the toes of another person.)

Inflammation- One of the oldest cures known to man civilized or savage- to reduce inflammation, poultice it with warm cow dung, or other semi-liquid dung. It is also good to draw a boil to a head.

Kidney Disease- This complaint may be cured by using goat urine.

Measles- Make and drink a mixture of sheep dung in water to produce a rash in measles or scarlet fever.

Mustache- If you would like your mustache to grow, put sweet milk or cream on your lip and let the cat lick it off. Sap of grapevines may do the same thing.

Mumps- It was a common practice to persuade one afflicted with mumps, to enter a pig-sty, and rub the swollen neck a certain odd-number of times on the front edge of the hog-trough, which was worn smooth by necks of the feeding swine.

Nosebleed- In modern times, for nosebleed, one can chew newspaper. Another cure: Try to recall who sat next to you the last time you were in church (IF you can!)

Piles- Potatoes, or horse chestnuts, carried in your pants-pockets are said to be good for this condition.

POPULAR HOME REMEDIES AND SUPERSTITIONS

Rheumatism- For rheumatism wear the eye-tooth of a pig; or carry three potatoes; or the triangular bone of a ram; or put a copper cent into your shoe; wear a ring made from a horseshoe nail; or a brass ring. Put glass knobs under the bed posts. Tie a dried eelskin around your joints. Carry a coffin nail. A salt mackerel tied on the feet cures. Carry a horse chestnut. Carry anything you want to- or, don't you have rheumatism?

Scratch or Cut- You can sterilize a wound by sucking it with your mouth; or, if not, if you can urinate on it; this also sterilizes.

Avoiding Sickness- Do not pay the doctor, at least in full, if you would avoid sickness in the family. Eating hailstones prevents fever.

Snake Bite- Catch a toad and tie it on the wound, to cure snake bite. If the toad dies, repeat the operation until the toad remains alive. Some believe that a toad, supposed to be poisonous in itself, if applied to cancer, will suck out the poison of the disease and thus cause a cure. (During the world war it was discovered that wounded men left for dead on the battlefield, often were covered with maggots, and recovering, too. Science has now come to develop the art of curing certain diseases, by letting the maggots do the work. Science, we will note, is often but the development of heretofore silly and simple home remedies and analogies.)

Sneezing- You can stop it if you look at the tip of your nose with both eyes; or press you index finger hard below your nose.

Sore Throat- Wear one of your long stockings around your neck, with the foot under the chin. This is good for head colds, too. Or, drag your finger between your toes and inhale deeply.

POPULAR HOME REMEDIES AND SUPERSTITIONS

Sprain- Should you have a sprain, or dislocation, rub them downward.

Tumor- If you have a tumor or other threatening growth, stroke same with the hand of a corpse, (we know of cases), and it will disappear with the decomposition of the corpse. (The English and Germans as well, believe that a birthmark can be eliminated by the same rule.)

Warts- Rub warts with pebbles and throw them into a grave; or rub warts with the blood of a chicken which has nothing but black feathers; or a piece of potato, which must then be buried under the eaves; or use soft green walnuts; or a hand of a corpse; or beans; or the head of a rooster that has just been killed; or the rind of bacon, which then hang on a tree so the birds may eat it. Pow wowers use saliva. Scratch a wart with a nail taken from a coffin, until the wart bleeds; it will then disappear.

Whooping Cough- Nearly every child gets it sooner or later, so a cure: put a live trout into the child's mouth; then, while still alive, put it back into the stream. (Some require the trout to breathe three times into the mouth of the child.) A trout or other small live fish, passed through the mouth of a slobbering baby, returned alive to the stream, is said to work wonders.

"Wind"- To break wind freely, if you have been sick in bed for a time, is a good sign. (Nurses tell us that they watch for this and other signs of recovery.)

HAVE GOOD LUCK - AVOID BAD LUCK

Belief in good, or bad luck, goes so far back into the history of man, that it, too, like other things in life, may be traced to the Pagan. Luck has a hold on the imagination of man today almost as great as ever. Men are inclined to blame nearly all our circumstances on our "bad luck"- or credit to "good luck." We hardly ever take time out to figure just what has "caused the effect, or result."

Test your friends and acquaintances on their belief or disbelief in various forms of "luck." Do our men today believe more in "luck," than women? The people of the rural sections in the years gone by have contributed to this rich lore, and we have no doubt that the believer and the unbeliever will alike get some pleasure from this catalog:

Bad Luck:

You should never sew anything while a person is wearing it.

You shouldn't step on a grating or cellar door in a pavement.

Don't kill a spider.

When two friends or acquaintances are walking together, nothing should be allowed to come between them.

When you start out, don't turn back to get that which you had forgotten- unless you sit down for a moment.

This one is as old as the hills: You will have a bad day of it if you get up with your left foot first. Always put the right foot on the floor first.

If you jump out of bed immediately on getting awake you will have a fall during the day. (Recently the medical journals suggested that one lie about twenty minutes before arising! Folklore is ages ahead of science, in many ways.)

Don't sew anything on Sunday; Ascension day, or other holy days.

POPULAR HOME REMEDIES AND SUPERSTITIONS

Bastard Child- A whistling girl, or one of easy virtue, will surely have a bastard child. (We know of mothers of fine families and breeding who forbid their daughters the "pleasure" of whistling.)

"Whistling girls and crowing hens come to a bad end."

Bed- You want to retain your beauty, so, take off and put on your stockings and shoes in bed.

You will get a sound rest if you place your bed due north and south. The Jews interpret a verse in the Psalms to read that "if the bedstead of any married couple stands with the head to the north and the feet to the south, the children begotten thereon will be all sons." The Englishman, Lord Beaverbrook, carries a compass, so that every strange bed in which he expects to lie, may be properly "pointed" before he retires.

Good housewives make the beds in the morning; lazy ones at noon; slatterns and pigs at night!

To Wet the Bed- If you want to have fun apply warm water to the feet of a sleeping person- it will make him wet the bed; or. dipping his hand into warm water will have the same effect- (or isn't this "fun?")

Bible- If you carry the 91st Psalm with you in the army, bullets will not harm you.

Carelessness- Many of us have seen a person stumble, and go back and start over again.

Charms- The Germans believe that they can protect their homes with the displaying of a "Himmelsbrief" (Letter of Protection). The Catholics have the same effect with their crucifix and holy water, and the Jews with their sacred word on the doorposts.

POPULAR HOME REMEDIES AND SUPERSTITIONS

Devil- If a bat flies into your house it is a sure sign the devil is after you- don't neglect having your screens put in place in time.

If you look into a mirror at night guess what you'll see? the "devil's rump."

Dog- If you don't want any visitors don't let the dog roll on the floor.

Ear- When your left ear burns you know that someone is speaking evil of you; if the right, they speak good- you know it.

Eye- If the right eye itches, it may mean you will see something agreeable, or have a lot of fun; when its the left eye, you have something to cry about.

Fire- If a woman can kindle a good fire she will be able to get a good husband. But he shouldn't take advantage of her accomplishment.

Good Luck- Carry a four-leaf clover, good for almost everything. Certain charms, blessed or otherwise; a rabbit's foot; potatoes, horse chestnuts, magic words written on parchment, are recognized as "good luck" charms.

A large wife and a large barn bring luck to any man.

Did you ever notice that most of the old barns in rural Pennsylvania were of generous proportions, although quite often the women were worn to shreds bearing children and helping to keep the barn filled with the necessities of life for man and beast.

They say: "Fools for luck, and the poor for children."

Kissing- When a girl recklessly puts on a man's hat it is an old-time belief that she wants a kiss. Our recollections of this belief, at parties, especially, is that she got it- and more; particularly if she had that personality and good looks which we lately have learned to know as "IT." But the girls were generally smart enough to pick out a certain hat, too!

Memory- To learn something by heart, put the book under the pillow when you go to bed; keep it closed. Leave a book lie open at night, and you will surely forget most that you have learned from it.

Money- It is nice to receive money before nine on Monday morning, for it means money coming in all week; but if you start to pay out before nine, you know what it means- paying out all the week.

Nose- If your nose itches, you will be kissed; or, you may get a letter. If your hand itches, rub it on wood.

Old Maid- Whoever eats the last piece of bread, you guessed it, will be an old maid.

Points- It doesn't always follow that if you hand a friend a pointed object with the point first, that it will break the friendship, although many believe it will bring bad luck; some people will not accept gifts with points unless they are permitted to "pay" for them, with a cent, or some small token.

Quarrel- Two persons using the same water to wash in may quarrel unless the one who washes last takes the necessary precaution to spit into the water- (before using it?) A quarrel may come if two persons wipe on the same towel, unless the one using it last, takes the trouble to turn it.

Want to start a family fight- play with a door, swinging it back and forth; or just twirl a chair too long.

Salt- If you spill salt, look out for a quarrel; to prevent, throw some over the left shoulder, or burn some of it.

Sneezing- Sneeze before breakfast, and you have a good sign of company coming that day. If you sneeze in bed, someone will come or depart within a day.

Telling Lies- Why do we get "pimples" on the tongue we've told an untruth. To get rid of it- spit three times into the fire.

Visitors- A man comes when a fork drops; if a knife, look for a woman. But if the butcher knife falls- look out- it will be the preacher. A teaspoon indicates disappointment. When a large spoon falls a braggart or an impudent person will appear.

Wedding- They say it is a sign of a wedding when a dog slides on his rump- but the sign must come from another cause, too. (No?)

Wishbone- Perhaps the reason they had a cradle to rock, was because one of them got the short end of the wishbone!

It may cause pain or stitches in the side to stir anything with a knife.

If fences are to last longer, the nails used in making them are to be dipped in oil.

Sometime when you pick something up from the street you may be sorry, or surprised- it may have been used in pow-wowing.

A blow on the "crazy bone" is as distressing as the loss or death of one's husband.

It is common to say: "Whatever happens the second time, will happen the third time."

POPULAR HOME REMEDIES AND SUPERSTITIONS

Should you feel that you have too many sons in succession, name one Adam, and the next child will be a girl!

Some one is thinking of you and may want to talk to you, if you hair pins persist in coming out.

Don't drop your dish cloth- it is a sign of slovenliness- either yourself, or someone coming, or leaving.

Because gypsies practiced various forms of deception they were believed to be able to do things other people couldn't. (But could they, really?)

"Cold hands and a warm heart."

Take hold of the big toe of a person talking in his sleep and he will tell you anything he knows- like one hypnotized.

Do not turn the wheels of a wagon, or buggy, backwards, while greasing, etc., or they will have a breakdown, or cause witches to bother you.

Recall the story of the horse: "If a sorrel is not tricky, its owner is."

FORM HABITS IN DRESSING AND SEWING

If a man or woman reaches the age of thirty, he or she will have had more than 10,000 chances to dress in the morning. By that time one should have become accustomed to the habit one way or another in dress, in toilet, in eating breakfast and attending to other matters natural in the course of an advancing day. Note, then, what one should do for good luck:

On arising mornings, clothe the right foot first to prevent quarreling during the day.

POPULAR HOME REMEDIES AND SUPERSTITIONS

It is luckier to put on both stockings first, and then shoes. Tearing off a button when dressing in the morning is a bad omen.

Accidentally putting on the stocking wrong side out mean? a present, or good luck, but unlucky to turn them on discovering the mistake.

If anyone sews or mends anything while he (or she) has it on, he will sew trouble on.

You will have cause to feel ashamed if you put on your shoes before putting on your trousers.

If one wears a new suit for the first time when going to church, or on a Sunday, it will wear twice as long.

WEATHER "FORECASTING" IS IMPORTANT

What, if anything; was more important to a farmer in the early days of our history, than an understanding of the probable state of the weather, not only for the morrow, but for a year or more in advance. Crops depended on favorable weather; they had to be rotated for successful farming. Most natural then, that we have our almanacs covering the weather forecast, signs of the zodiac, phases of the sun, moon and other planets; the religious and civil special days. Long range weather forecasts are said to be substantially as reliable over a period of time as the government forecast.

February 2 has been widely advertised as "Ground-hog Day." It has two other designations: 1. "Woodchuck Day," a better term than the former, (some say); and, 2. "Candlemas"- an ecclesiastical festival held in honor of the presentation of the infant Christ in the temple and the purification of the Virgin Mary.

In Pennsylvania, particularly, the coming of "Ground-hog day" is looked forward to with some anticipation. When this little prophet appears from his "home," should he see his shadow, he returns promptly, and all the world may take due and timely notice that six weeks of winter will endure. (In some sections four weeks is the rule.) In many rural sections men of small stature are expected, or chided to remain indoors on this date if the weather is clear, so as not to unduly tempt the forces of nature which control the balance of winter.

Generally animals of every sort and description may be used in foretelling the weather, being something man has had about him for centuries, observing their ways and habits.

Animals used in forecasting include: The ass (four-legged variety), beaver, bear, bull, cat, cattle, chipmunk, deer, dog, donkey, fox, ground-squirrel, goat, hog, horse, mole, mouse, muskrat, ox, rabbit, rat, sheep and wolf, etc.

Birds of all sorts, as well as trees, shrubs and grasses; even fish; also clouds, fog and frost; insects; the moon, sun and stars.

We can foretell weather for all seasons of the year in many ways. For instance:

Cat- A cat lying on its side and turning its face upward foretells stormy weather.

Caterpillar- The color of the caterpillar foretells the severity of the winter; if the ends are black, the beginning and the end of winter will be hard; if the middle, then the middle of winter.

Chickens- If chickens molt on the forepart of the body first, then the early part of winter will be severe; if on the rear, then the end of winter.

POPULAR HOME REMEDIES AND SUPERSTITIONS

Corn- Thick husk on corn foretells a hard winter; if the husk is so short that the ears protrude, the winter will be mild.

Corns- Aching corns are a sign of rain.

Days- As is the weather on the fifth day of the month, so it will be the rest of the month; as the last Friday, so the following month.

Dog- A dog lying on its back indicates a change to stormy weather.

Food- If all the food on the table is eaten the saying is: "Tomorrow will be a clear day."

Goosebone- About the breastbone of a goose: When held up to the light, if it shows dark upon the whole rather than otherwise, we shall have a severe winter throughout; if mottled variable, the lighter aspects betokening snow; the darker, frosts. The general transparency of the bone denotes an open winter, the front part foretelling the state of that season before Christmas, and the inner part the weather after Christmas.

Lightning- Never point your finger at lightning.

Pain- Pain in a scar or in one's bones indicates rain, or an early change in the weather.

Rain- Morning showers and old women's dancing do not last long.

Snow- The number of snows during winter is indicated by the number of days from the first snow in fall to the next following full moon; or the first of the following month.

Sound- If a clock with brass works ticks very loud, or if you can hear trains, bells, or whistles at a great distance, or smoke hangs low, it is a sign of stormy weather.

Trees- If the tops of trees are bare while the sides are still covered with leaves, the winter will be mild; if the leaves fall first from the sides, the winter will be severe.

WE EXAMINE SPECIAL DAYS AND SEASONS

The influence of the moon on tides, crops, love and the mind, has been recognized for centuries. Perhaps the old-fashioned notions that one could do a wrong in certain seasons or certain days, is really responsible for the custom of our men and women not wanting to break down these customs inherited from their forefathers, and presumably originally from the Jews, whose religion became the religion of the Christian. Today farmers will let foods rot in the fields rather than do a "lick" of work on Sunday. It isn't so much that the farmer is "religious" on Sunday that stops his work, as it is the "fear" of what might happen if he did.

He drives a nice team, or runs an automobile, and does many other things for his own personal pleasure on Sunday, but by no ordinary line of reasoning can you justify the "pleasure" angle, over that of working on the Sabbath if your crops need attention:

"Bright"- Christmas children are brighter than others they can hear and understand "cattle talk;" they can also see ghosts.

Cattle- Farmers should not clean stables between Christmas and New Year, if they want the cattle to live and thrive. Witches will interfere if this rule is violated.

Fishing- Ascension day is a day when one goes fishing, and our recollection is that young people, and older ones, too, did other things on this day- when they went "fishing." While on "fishing" let it be known that if a woman crosses your path when you go fishing, you might as well go home- you won't catch any fish. Before casting you should spit on your bait.

Friday- Never begin anything on that day, it is an unlucky day. Friday was said to be the Mohammedan Sabbath, by Divine command. The Moslem also believes that Friday was the day on which Adam was created, and received into Paradise, the day on which he was expelled from it, the day on which he repented and the day on which he died. It will, by the same sign, be the day of the resurrection. For a long while criminals were put to death on Friday- hence "hangman's" day.

Health- If you want to keep well, don't wash yourself, or take a bath, or even change clothing between Christmas and New Year. Even on New Year's day it is bad luck to change to a clean shirt; to do so may cause boils. New Year's day is a good day to eat sausage to keep you healthy throughout the year.

Plastering- Don't start to plaster a house on Saturday if you don't want the plastering to fall off.

Wednesday- This day is a poor washday; cattle may die, or bad luck come to those who wash on this day.

LAWS FOR THE FARMER AND WOODSMAN

If there was anyone among a number of groups among the Pennsylvania-Germans who was put more or less to his own resources it must have been the farmer and the woodsman. They had to depend on their own logic and line of reasoning in many cases where it was impossible to depend on book-learning, or any specific knowledge bordering on the scientific. While almanacs were to be had, covering many facts necessary to his work, time was several generations ago that no printed matter was available except the Bible and a few books on the law of the land. If we blame the early farmers for manners which to us seem foolish, do we want to declare that today we know everything there is to know that is worthwhile, and that we do things the right way? Hardly; so let the farmer do things his way.

Poultry and Eggs- Chickens hatched from eggs laid on Good Friday will be speckled. Eggs laid on Good Friday will not decay.

Eggs laid on Friday are used in "pow-wowing." It is not well to discuss the setting of hens at meal time, else the eggs will not hatch.

To insure a good hatch, set hens on Sunday between eleven and twelve, when the benediction is pronounced in church. Egg shells should be crushed before they are thrown away, else the witches will use them for boats.

This is a good rule: Carry a dead chicken beyond the confines of your premises to prevent others from dying- but be sure that you are not caught doing this "dirty" trick.

Trees- If a tree will not bear fruit, drive nails into it. Trees for building purposes should be foiled in December. When transplanting a tree, be careful to have the same side facing the south.

Wood from a tree struck by lightning should never be used in the construction of a house, or barn, or they in turn may also be struck by lightning.

Empty the pot at the peach tree, or "wet" against it, so that it will bear better.

If a pregnant woman helps plant a tree, if she takes hold of it with both hands the tree will bear doubly well.

You will become blind, so they say, if you look up into a

tree while a woman is on the tree.

Stock- When a cow aborts it is customary to bury the dead-born calf under the barn eaves, just outside the cowstable door.

To cure founder from over-feeding, urinate on the horse's fodder.

To cure colic or retention of urine in a horse, let a woodlouse crawl about the horse.

If you would prevent abortion in cows, hang a dog's skull in the cow-stable.

When ready to wean a calf, back it out of the stable and the cow will not low for it.

Pets- Cats and Dogs- Men, women and children quite often are fond of some form of animal or bird life. Our interests in them often correspond to affections we bear to children or other members of our own families. A person fond of dogs and cats will make a good husband or wife.

If you touch kittens before their eyes are open, the mother cat will let them starve.

Shoot a cat and your luck is gone.

To prevent a dog from running away feed him some bread which you have warmed in your arm pits.

Call a dog "water" or "fire" and he cannot be bewitched. Scratch a dog where he can't scratch himself and he won't run away.

"MUSTS" IN COOKING, BAKING, PLANTING

A more or less fixed idea that to do this or that on certain holy days is to sin, or be blessed, has its parallel in home-cooking or baking. Long before there were Pennsylvania-Germans, and long before there were Protestants or Catholics, there were the Jews who followed the laws of Moses, and who observed the day of rest, a day in which no cooking was allowed by one of their kind.

This is likewise true on others of the Jewish religious days, when food must be prepared thus and so, or when, on a certain day they are not allowed to eat of any beans or other food which might cause them to be "windy" on their special holiday. If our people do these things, surely it must needs be merely a frayed observance of what has been in the past, being done in our own good way and with our own good pleasure.

Baking- Ascension day- bread baked on this day will not become moldy.

Do not bake on Good Friday.

To make a cake bake light, always stir the batter the same direction.

Planting- Don't plant peas or beans on the day baking is done.

There is considerable belief that potatoes planted in the afternoon will not yield.

Transplanting parsley is risky. If a woman does this she may lose her husband, and have other bad luck.

Jesus lay buried from Good Friday to Easter, so no

gardening or planting should be done between those days.

For a good yield, plant peas and potatoes when the corners of the moon are up, i. e., in the increase.

If you want large cucumbers, have a man plant them.

Flowers- If you want nice, large plants, steal the slips. (Remember, stolen fruit always has the best taste.) Flower plants will be short and chunky, if you should happen to sit down right after planting them.

CARE OF THE TEETH KNOWN TO ANCIENTS

It was the custom in the dawn of history, at least of man, to eat what he could, when he could get his hands on anything. There was plenty of assurance that he would get plenty of exercise for his teeth and gums. Many of our old-fashioned beliefs come from times B. C. If teeth are picked by a splint of wood from a tree which was struck by lightning, the toothache will cease but the teeth will decay.

Cut your nails on Sunday, or Friday, to prevent toothache.

To aid dentition, rub a child's gums with rabbit's brain, before it is, however, six months old.

To prevent toothache you should, when washing your face, pass the hand full of water three times behind the ears.

Your teeth will decay if you eat anything at which rats have nibbled, or at which someone else has nibbled.

An extracted tooth should be put into the fire at once.

Spitting into the fire causes toothache.

POPULAR HOME REMEDIES AND SUPERSTITIONS

Other ways to stop toothache include: Putting on of the left stocking first; rubbing the tooth with a snakeskin; biting off a white dog turd; pick the tooth with a needle used in making a shroud, or with a coffin nail; put your coat on right side first; bury the parings of fingernails and toenails under the eaves on the north side of the house. One of the best known of these beliefs, (and well recalled by the editor when but a mere boy), is: "Mousey, mousey, I am giving you an old tooth, give me a new one in its stead."

MOON LORE FAMILIAR TO ALL PEOPLE

Before man was, there was the moon. This body, coming as it does at night to cast its soft beams on tender lovers, chicken thieves, and high-jackers, has its worshipers today as in the early days of man's history. Note how it affected our people in past years, as well as today If there is anything in folk-lore that goes back into remote times much further than "moon lore," we have no recollection of it at the moment. Besides going crazy over little or nothing at "full moon;" becoming moon-struck over someone you love; using the moon as part of your religion, etc., there are those who plant in this sign; cut their hair, and a thousand other things- all by the sign of the "moon."

Sweep the house in the dark of the moon and you will have neither moths nor spiders.

Fences built when the horns of the moon turn up will freeze out of the ground.

You will go crazy if the moon shines on you in bed, or perhaps your features will become distorted.

Corns should be cut in the wane of the moon (but should corns be "cut?")

Smoked meats should be taken out of the smoke house in

the dark of the moon to prevent them from becoming wormy. The meat of animals killed in the increase of the moon will not shrink in the pot or in curing.

Show the new moon money and you will have more.

If the new moon shines on fish or meat, they will spoil. Seeing the new moon for the first time over the left shoulder is unlucky.

DREAMS AND WHAT THEY MEAN TO US

This subject is one which is largely made up of an aurora of "elusiveness." One cannot pin down the dreams to anything factual- they may seem realistic. Dreams are supposed to represent "contraries"- opposites of what we dream.

Our experience in meeting the public from day to day tells us that too many people believe in dreams. If they devoted as much time to sound thinking as in trying to put their distorted dreams into effect, or if they tried to get away from hallucinations, we would assuredly be better off as a people.

The Pennsylvania-Germans come by their belief in dreams quite honestly, and you cannot blame them for it, if sometimes their interpretations do not come true. There is probably some good reason for dreams, but it seems like common sense advice to dreamers not to place too much confidence in dreams!

Relate the dream before breakfast and it will come true.

If you dream of falling you will commit sin.

To dream of a funeral means a wedding.

Dream of milk and you will fall violently in love.

POPULAR HOME REMEDIES AND SUPERSTITIONS

Dreaming of eggs indicates a quarrel.

Dreaming of muddy water means trouble or a death.

It is a good omen to dream of the dead- it may foretell of a wedding.

What you dream the first night you are in a strange house will come true (if you can get to sleep the first night).

What you dream on Friday night will come true.

To dream of snakes means enemies.

Dreaming of a runaway is a sign of rain. (Now that we have so few horses, and so many automobiles, we cannot use this old method; however, we can depend on rain if the official government weather forecast calls for "fair.")

WITCHES AND OUR OWN SUPERSTITIONS

Death and hell are perhaps the only things man fears more than witches. Nothing has come down through time that has harmed man's mind so much as these "unseen things in the dark." Briefly, some notions are recalled to US, as follows:

Borrowing- If you think you are bewitched, beware of the first person coming to borrow from you- it is the witch!

Broom- If you are bewitched lay a broom before the door. The "rules" decree that the first person to come in, and to pick up the broom, is the witch.

Witches ride brooms. Brooms are used to sweep out the witches.

Black Cat- The black cat is the most prevalent form of a

witch. (This is evident today when we fear the consequences which may follow if a black cat crosses our path.)

Egg-Shells- They should always be burned or crushed into small bits, to prevent chickens being bewitched. (Another idea traceable to the early Jews.)

Gun- For a gun that is bewitched, stick two pins on it in the form of a cross. (Witches and devils hate crosses, which, as we know, are weapons or charms handed down to us from the early Christian church.)

A witch cannot "make her water" until she seeks to be forgiven, if you are willing to lay a bewitched gun in a creek.

Shirt- Cut both sleeves out of a husband's shirt and burn them to discover who the witch is. (How it is done we don't profess to know.)

Soap- If a woman comes along while you are boiling soap, the soap will be bewitched.

The Pennsylvania-German belief in witches comes indirectly from the Hebrews or Jews, for these witches were invented or created in the Old Testament. This compilation is so difficult for the layman to understand, that most of his sins can be attributed to his distant relationship with the Old Testament authority and the poor layman's inability to interpret, or cope with this vast authority; hence he flounders about in a maze that challenges the honest opinions of the learned even of the clergy. So if the poor P.-G. Believes in witches don't blame him; if he goes to church, he gets them without the real truth to digest them; if he is a non church-goer, his interpretation is still more involved.

Common among our people is the belief that a witch will not step over a broomstick.

POPULAR HOME REMEDIES AND SUPERSTITIONS

Fasten a sprig of St. John's wort to the door to keep out witches or flies.

Nail a toad's foot over the stable door to drive and keep the witches out of the stable.

Cut off the ears (sacrifice of the O.T.) of a black cat, burn them and feed the ashes to the witch.

If bread won't rise, it is bewitched.

To discover a witch: draw a picture of the suspect, load your gun with a dime, and shoot at the picture. The spot where you hit the picture will correspond to the mark to be found on the body of the witch.

If there is a witch in the house throw a handful of coarse salt into the fire with the left hand.

When a child is bewitched pull its shirt over the head wrong side out and wedge the sleeves or clothes behind the door.

Load a bewitched gun with a bullet of hair.

When the witch disappears, a black cat appears. (The witch and the black cat appeared in a witch-shooting in Schuylkill county, Penna., some years ago; a bewitched boy shot an old woman, he claimed had him bewitched; Exodus xxii 18, accommodates one with authority for getting rid of witches)

IDEAS FOR GETTING A FUTURE HUSBAND

The chances of catching a man for a husband these days are so much better than they were several generations ago. The ease with which one can meet another person, and our convenient transportation system breaks down the need for some of the notions held by our mothers and grandmothers. However, we do know that fortune-tellers and other means are still employed by our sweet dames, and they still do believe in dreams.

Blood- Many contracts are signed and sealed in blood. A drop of it taken from the little ringer of the left hand of a man, put into a glass of water given to a girl to drink, is supposed to cause her to fall in love with the donor of the blood.

Cat- A girl should feed a cat from her shoe if she once gets pretty anxious to marry.

Feathers- Fine feathers around the house "for nice," discourage suitors for the hand of "proud" girls living there.

Hearts- If you can arrange to kiss a girl while you secrete a heart of a turtle-dove in your mouth, it will act as a love charm- no one can be sure of what may happen as a result.

Try to swallow a raw chicken heart; the man you are thinking of at the time will be your future husband.

Marriage- If a clergyman should marry two couples on the same day, one of them will be unhappy.

Shirt- Years ago a sensible girl wouldn't think of getting married until she could make a man's shirt. Today, most young women can neither make a man's shirt, nor cook a decent meal, unless it comes from cans and needs heating only; few can concoct tasty dishes from ideas in their own heads, or even with the aid of a good cook book.

Shoes- In olden days a girl kept on her new shoes the first time she wore them; the man who came to take them off was to be the new husband. But many a girl was left to remove her own shoes.

POPULAR HOME REMEDIES AND SUPERSTITIONS

Skirt- Sometimes we see a woman with her skirt turned up the back- she has a lover who is a widower.

If you see a bramble, or "boova lice," on a woman's skirt, it not only indicates she has a lover, but... she probably was out for a "friendly walk" with him.

Sugar- Put some sugar under the armpits until it gets warm- it will act as an aphrodisiac if you put it into a drink which you should offer to the girl who spurns your attentions. (But never tell her afterward of your method, should you be fortunate enough to win her over.)

MARRIAGE LORE AND NATURAL TRENDS

One of the earliest institutions of man was the arrangement of man to marry a woman. He was obliged to take an oath before God, making this a high and significant act. The politicians early in history got the church to permit them to share in this highly attractive proposition, and now both profit well from the small initial investment, for license and consummation by clergy, judge, justice of the peace, or the sea captain- Resulting progeny are taxed doubly- once by the state and again by the church. If the first isn't paid, you cannot own property, and may go to jail; if the second isn't paid, you may be ex- communicated, and perchance- or probably, will go to... the bad place

Marry in something borrowed.

To meet a priest, hare, cat, dog, lizard or serpent on going to church to be married are considered unlucky.

A laughing bride becomes a weeping wife.

As the weather on the wedding-day, so the married life. Changing one's wedding clothes before night brings bad luck.

POPULAR HOME REMEDIES AND SUPERSTITIONS

You will have no luck if you make your own trousseau.

The first to go to bed, or to go to sleep on the wedding night will be the first to die. (Suppose neither should happen to fall asleep that night? After all, most of us marry but once, and a honeymoon might keep a couple awake all night!)

A man should wear on his wedding day a shirt his bride gave him.

To have luck in married life, or to prevent being bewitched (they are synonymous), a married couple should step over a broom on entering their house.

If a woman objects to a man's advances he should crawl three times under a brier which has taken second root.

SEX-LORE AND PRE-NATAL "INFLUENCES"

There is all too little material written and published concerning the rights and privileges of man and woman who have taken the marriage vow, and placed in the proper hands.

That children should be told year after year, that the doctor goes to the creek, or to a spring, and there gets his stock of babies for delivery to a prospective mother, in the opinion of many, is too thin. It is unnecessary deception, and, in our opinion, is as silly and foolish, and unnecessary as the case of the woman who nursed her son until he was old enough to chop wood for her cook stove needs! She actually made him chop for his dinner!

Children learn to lie quick enough, without "well meaning" parents telling them additional lies, because they had these same lies told to them, and who today are prudes without knowing it.

POPULAR HOME REMEDIES AND SUPERSTITIONS

Eating anything that has grown double will cause twins.

If a woman plays a musical instrument during her pregnancy, her offspring will be musical; or, if she is cheerful, her children will be good natured.

If a man visits a woman during confinement and his hat is thrown on the bed, it will not be returned to him until he has given a present for the newborn child.

If a doctor is not fully paid when a woman is about to be confined she will be in difficult labor.

A woman will not have chloasma if she wipes her face with the first diaper wetted by her newborn child. (We have it from several different sources, that this is common in Perry county, Pa.)

Sauerkraut will spoil if made by a woman in her periods. (The Jews were particular about women and their periodic uncleanness). Radishes and onions do not agree with a woman in her periods; or, if she plays with a dog during such time, she will be bitten by the dog. A woman should not boil soap, nor do any baking during menstruation; at such times fruit put up by her will not keep.

A woman should not take off her wedding ring during confinement, else witches will have power over her. If a pregnant woman passes under a washline her child will have a birth mark; likewise, it might wind the umbilical cord about her offspring's neck. If a woman is frightened by anything during her pregnancy her offspring will have a birthmark.

MOVING, OR "FLITTIN'" DAY

As moving is something that falls to the lot of the majority of people in the course of a life time, there is a wealth of lore relative to changing from place to place.

Moving- Friday flittings- short sittings.

Never take an old broom while moving.

Leaving something behind when removing is a lucky omen.

Never take eggs with you when moving.

A child should be given some cold water immediately after moving to prevent its becoming homesick.

Keep a stray cat after moving- good luck.

Don't take the cat with you the day you move; its bad luck. Fetch her later.

DEATH AND HOW TO "CIRCUMVENT" IT

Few people really want to die. Being the one thing all must meet in time, we postpone the day by every means at our physical and mental disposal. Fancied experiences in years past have contributed to these beliefs, with many others, but no laws have yet been passed which will overcome what to some people are utterly ridiculous notions. Here we have them

Changing Rooms- A sick person will die if changed from one room to another.

Death Omens- If cracks appear in bread while baking; whining of a dog beneath a window; a picture falling from the wall; if a cricket gets into the house; a sick person pulling at the bedclothes; if you miss a row while planting; a child crying while being baptized; if horses neigh at a funeral; sneezing at the table; counting the conveyances at a funeral- all of these are omens of death.

Do not erect a tombstone in less than a year after a death, else there will be another in the family, soon.

Drowning- If the body of a drowned person cannot be found, throw a loaf of bread into the water. If the body is anywhere nearby, the bread will hover about.

Eyes- The open eyes of a corpse are looking for the next one to follow.

New Year's Day- A perfect calm on the first day of the year means many old people will die during the year. The same holds good when, in the north, Christmas comes in "green."

Shirt- Always wash a new shirt before wearing; for if you are taken sick in an unwashed one, you will never get well.

Thirteen- This number sitting down to a meal- one of them will die within a year. (Goes back to the Last Supper.)

"OMENS" ABOUT DEATHS AND FUNERALS

Sometimes we are glad when some of our neighbors "pass away," but generally not in our own immediate families. There is something in Christian religions and homes which erects a fear about incidents connected with funerals. Is this stimulated by the old fashioned sermons dealing with "life after death, in a fiery place?" Man unconsciously harbors his fears, but indicates his attitude in his manifestations on many occasions, none the least of them when he is challenged to "think" about his possibilities and probabilities of dying before he has time to make good with his Maker for the sins he has committed, or thinks he did. The interesting lore of our people finds them also involved with superstition and lore relative to deaths and funerals.

POPULAR HOME REMEDIES AND SUPERSTITIONS

They are never to count the number of vehicles in a funeral procession- it prophesys bad luck- but this is one weakness of our people, particularly if there is a large attendance.

All jewelry should be taken from the corpse before burial.

If there are many deaths in a family in rapid succession, the grave of the first of those to die should be opened, to see whether the corpse has not drawn a part of its shroud into its mouth.

Move the bee-hive When the funeral leaves the house to prevent the bees from dying or becoming worthless. (Bees and honey are scriptural).

Smelling at flowers which grow on a grave, or have lain in a coffin will destroy the sense of smell.

If anyone in a funeral procession looks back, there will soon be another funeral.

Relative to making death come easy: take away the pillow of the sick person; or, unlock all locks, doors, drawers, etc. Stop the clock, and the end will soon come. Open the windows in the death chamber immediately after death so that the soul can get out. Mirrors should be covered with crepe immediately after a death; shining objects covered with cloths, and the clock stopped and shrouded over to show that with him time is over. Pictures should be turned to the wall.

If it rains or snows into a grave the dead will go to heaven.

A light, or candle is frequently burned in the room where the corpse reposes until the day of burial. (When the Germans do this, they emulate the Catholic, who, whether he knows it or not, is emulating the Jew).

BIBLIOGRAPHY

We present a good working' list of titles having to do with source material on the "home remedies" and "superstitions" of the Pennsylvania Germans. There are others, not to forget to mention Albertus Magnus' "Egyptian Secrets," and "Sixth and Seventh Books of Moses." Possession of these two titles, and Hohmah's "Long Lost Friend," is generally a more or less "professionally" guarded "secret." Although these books have been on the market for upwards of a hundred years, they continue to be among the "best-seller" class in many stores throughout the country.

Aurand, A. Monroe, Jr. Little Known Facts About the Ritual of the Jews and the Esoteric Folklore of the Pennsylvania-Germans. 8vo 108pp Harrisburg, Pa., 1939.

Aurand, A. Monroe, Jr. The "Pow Wow" Book; A Treatise on the Art of "Healing by Prayer" and "Laying on of Hands," etc. p. x, 85. Contains also: An Account of the "Witch" Murder Trial, York, Pa., Jan. 7-9, 1929; also: John George Hohman's Pow-Wows; or Long Lost Friend; A Collection of Mysterious and Invaluable Arts and Remedies, p. 64. indexed.

Brendle, Thomas R., and Unger. Claude W. Folk Medicine of the Pennsylvania Germans. The non-occult cures. 8Vo 303pp Norristown, Pa., 1935. (Vol. XLV of the Penna.-German Society Proceedings.)

Fisher, H. L. Olden Times: or, Pennsylvania Rural Life, Some Fifty Years Ago, and Other Poems. Illus. 8vo 472pp indexed. York, Pa.. 1888.

Fogel, Edwin Miller. Beliefs and Superstitions of the

POPULAR HOME REMEDIES AND SUPERSTITIONS

Pennsylvania Germans. 8vo 387pp Philadelphia 1915.

Gibbons, Phoebe Earle. "Pennsylvania Dutch" and Other Essays. 12mo 427pp. Phila. v.d.

Grumbine, Dr. E. Folk-Lore and Superstitious Beliefs of Lebanon County, (p. 254-294, in Lebanon County Historical Society Proceedings, vol. III.)

Home, A. R. Home's Pennsylvania German Manual. 12Mo 372pp Allentown 1910.

Kuhns, Oscar. The German and Swiss Settlements of Colonial Pennsylvania. A study of the so-called Penna.-Dutch. 12mo 268pp indexed New York 1900, 1914 (now published by The Aurand Press, Harrisburg, Pa.)

Americana Germanica. Univ. of Penna. Monographs. Pennsylvania-German Magazine, (and Penn-Germania), 1900-1914. Pennsylvania German Society Proceedings.

THE END